Ghost Passage

Josephine Balmer

Ghost Passage

Shearsman Books

First published in the United Kingdom in 2022 by
Shearsman Books Ltd
PO Box 4239
Swindon
SN3 9FN

Shearsman Books Ltd Registered Office
30–31 St. James Place, Mangotsfield, Bristol BS16 9JB
(this address not for correspondence)

www.shearsman.com

ISBN 978-1-84861-794-0

Contents

ACKNOWLEDGEMENTS

Poems have previously appeared in *Agenda, Arion, ARTEMISpoetry, Ink, Sweat & Tears, New Statesman, One Hand Clapping, Poetry Salzburg Review* and *The Interpreter's House*. Grateful thanks are due to the editors of these volumes.

Many of the poems from 'In Wood' were written for a joint project with the London Mithraeum museum and the University of Notre Dame (USA) in England. Several were performed by students of Notre Dame at the London Mithraeum Bloomberg Space in November 2019 as part of the national Being Human Festival. Thanks are due to Joseph Andrews, Gabrielle Evans and Jay Skelton of Notre Dame, Roger Tomlin, and Helen Chiles of the London Mithraeum for hosting the event. Above all, I am indebted to Charlotte Parkyn of Notre Dame for her unfailing enthusiasm and unflappable support for the project.

Profound thanks are also due to Fiona Macintosh and Lorna Hardwick of Classics and Poetry Now, Laura Swift of The Art of Fragments, Susanne Turner and Justyna Ladosz of the Cast Gallery, Cambridge, Eliana Maestri of the Centre for Translating Cultures, Exeter, Efi Spentzou of the Centre for Reception of Greece and Rome, London, Emily Hauser and Helena Taylor of Women Creating Classics, Dominic Rathbone, Helen Lovatt, Hugh Bowden, Lesley Saunders, Liam Guilar, Alan Humm, and Tony Frazer – and all those who kept the conversations on poetry going throughout a difficult few years but especially Fiona Cox, Elena Theodorakopoulos and Paschalis Nikolaou for their generous responses and incisive contributions. I am grateful, as ever, to my husband Paul Dunn for reading the drafts.

Everything in the landscape is older than we think… for a moment or two we succeed in entering into the minds of the dead.
    W.G. Hoskins, *The Making of the English Landscape*

This is the book of a city which will not be destroyed…
    Arthur Mee, *The King's England: London* (1948 edition)

Writer [?], London

Writing tablets, Walbrook, London

It seems a slip, a novice error,
marked as if crossed through.
A name no one can read. Or knew.

But I am the first. It holds my fear
and my life, the heart-knot terror
of a letter misplaced, misconstrued.
I breathe through its blocked lungs –
my blood, my bone, my sinew.

And all those others yet to come.
Centuries later fold back each leaf
to trace the fossil frail we'll make,
this usury of borrowed tongues;
mud-stopped loans, gains of dust,
the lines we send like ash-bud moths
to brush your doorstep as you sleep:
We bear witness in our own hand
that debts owed shall be paid later...

We have seen our city shrink to sand
so we scratch wood to soothe the ache –
diminished words we leave behind
to score these shuddering, ghosted streets
back into form and place: *London writer.*

Then hand them on for you to shape.

I.

In Wood

What London hath been of ancient time men may here see, as
what it is now every man doth behold…
(John Stow, *A Survey of London*, 1508)

Cicero (Minor) Conquers Britain

Southern Britain, September, 54 BCE

Caesar… tells me you were not yet with him
when he reached the coast

As usual I was following in the rear.

My brother teased about the chariots
I could buy for souvenirs. Or the lack
of bookish Britons to trade as slaves.
He talked of turned tides, of steeper
cliffs to scale than my stalled career.

Riding back to the sea from inland
I'd found subdued villages, smoke
scrolled up like fading stylus strokes;
neat fields crossed by tangled hedges,
hardly touched by our war. Oblivious.

From Rome Marcus wrote of the heat,
of roof repairs, plumbing, land prices;
of savage words bartered in the senate,
ambition pressed between pine tablets
as he boasted of each winning speech.

In my deep lanes, the blossom turned
like soured milk; dog roses gave way
to dark thorns, scarlet berries. Waves
of parsley parted, foaming as I passed.
Alder shivered with each drop of rain.

I abandoned the tragedy I was writing.
My talents wouldn't match my temper;
I saw its ending, each sharp, staged death.
I was never in the centre, only at the edge.
On the losing side. And to my brother.

The First European
Legionary tomb, Colchester, 49 CE

They never managed to pronounce my name;
as I'm tall, I was always 'Longinus',
'Lofty' (I'm Sdapeze, son of Matygus,
a Thracian from Sofia). Can't complain:
I was on double time. The days were dank
but the oysters were good. I bought a cloak
plus a fine hunting bitch, Agassia,
with squat little legs, sharp teeth and soft paws.
The wife and kids back home would have loved her.

Fifteen years I served with the cavalry
across the east – Syria, Scythia.
At forty it ends here. Remember me:
I was in the advance, one of the first.
Your ancestor. My bones still feed this earth.

Pecking Orders

Writing tablet, Walbrook, London, 51 CE

To Titus Birdface, Poultry man…

A word of caution in your own interest
through the City, debtors are crowing
that your new bills are ever-flowing;

if you ruffle feathers, bring discredit,
no one here will thank you for it –
you won't advance by these advances

only undermine our fledgling markets.
Such loans are more than we'll allow.
So heed this warning: don't play foul.

That night I could have heard stars touch,
the sigh of fish through the quicksilver river.
Yet somehow, I swear, I missed my latch

lifting, the spite-soft step of 'Anonymous'
slipping their sour tablet beneath my door.
A month ago, in Athens, I was in the agora

debating Plato by moonlight, Pythagoras.
Here, in Britain, they waste good wax
and wood on weak puns, vindictiveness.

These are the paltry men. Chicken feed.
We Greeks do not care for pecking orders.
I will lay my nest eggs where I please.

In the Second Consulship of Nero

Writing tablet, Walbrook, London, 8 January, 57 CE

I, Tibullus, freedman of Venustus,
owe 105 denarii to Gratus, freedman
of Spurius, for goods sold and delivered…

I knew it was a gamble, rash even.
But the year was fresh, the month of Janus –
the god of openings, gateways, passages.
And I believe, like my fellow freedmen,
that the way it starts is the way it ends.

We didn't choose to come. We were baggage –
stateless, nameless – of our former master
(who'd half-read the poet I'm called after).
Yet we found shelter here, security,
a place to bank our safe new currency,
the ceaseless tap, tap, tap of builders' tools
countered by scratch, scratch, scratch of IOUs.

Soon Nero will abolish all taxes.
This town is booming. Our fortunes with it.

Destruction Horizon
Walbrook, London, 60 CE

...to save a province, Suetonius sacrificed a city....

On the streets, priests spoke of omens,
babbling voices in the lock-down basilica,
laughter rattling out from empty theatres,
a twin city reflected in the rising Thames.

I didn't waver. We didn't have the numbers.
I gave the command to march on. Some came.
Most were trapped by age or sex, a strange
allegiance to this border post, a tenderness
for hovels they somehow held as home.
They saw the dust storm spinning nearer,
carrying their own deaths – and the British.
A tally of thousands for that bitch Boudica.

But we left them a marker in memorial,
our destruction horizon: impacted soil,
a trickle of crimson soot like dried blood.
Dig down. Dig deep. It's soaked in the mud.

New Roman

Writing tablet, Walbrook, London, 61 CE

ABCDEFGHIKL
MNOPQRST...

In a charred shack we learn our lessons.

Through the smoke I can smell sorrel, ramsons,
blackthorn blossom drifting across like ash
as the shouts of soldiers shatter our hush
and wagons of the dead still roll on past.

We do not want this world, the old language:
destruction, put to fire, revolt, flight, death.
Our task is to etch a new alphabet –
new letters, new tools to rebuild our homes,
gardens for us children, games to play, schools.
We'll smooth the jagged edge of dialect
and salve its gaping wounds in majuscule.

A-B-C: the scorched march of New Roman
turning blackened wood into cold white stone.

Enumeration

Writing tablet, Walbrook, London, 62 CE

l)) ((l))
l)) ((l)) ((l))
l)) ((l)) ((l)) ((l))
l)) ((l)) ((l)) ((l)) ((l))

Letters gained, we reckoned up the numbers.

We copied the strokes to make our totals,
adding in brackets to each vertical:
((l)) = ten thousand; (((l))) = ten times more.
During the revolt, the Romans had sneered
that we British were merely amateurs
with no grasp of the hard commerce of war:
slaves, ransoms, trafficking. That we measured
our victories not in profit but gore.

We took the correction. To be truthful,
before they taught us enumeration
we had no figures, no way to begin.
Now we've adopted their horizontal:
men out=conquest=taxation=monies in.

Provisions
Writing tablet, Walbrook, London, 21 October, 62 CE

I, Rennius Venustus, contract with Valerius Proculus
that he will transport twenty cartloads of provisions
at a quarter of one denarius each load from St Albans
to London by the Ides of November. On condition that…:

No payment will be made or compensation
given for road repair or gap in communication,
fire, flood, or act of war, especially rebellion.

A penalty will be exacted for any deadlines
passed or dispatch missed, as here defined
by an elbow's length, that is, half an arm.

The demands of the City will for now
outrank those of any other fort or town
so long as the price of food stays firm

and hunger holds against war-spoiled corn.

Backfill

Writing tablet, Walbrook, London, 64 CE

From Julius Classicus, Prefect
of the Sixth Cohort of Nervii

London suited me. We dug through bone
to rebuild streets the British had levelled,
unflinching when that sagittal hail rattled
down our faces until we wept stones.

They all feared I was too lazy, prone
to dissipation, drawing out my leisure
as if enjoying the fruits of an empire
I'd already won. They were all wrong.

After work I might have thrown dice
or drunk enough in Crispus's tavern.
Yet, voice soft, I still urged my men
to rip away those pleasures, the vice

by which we had been held subject
far more than mere force or numbers.
We Gauls, I said, have long memories
and our ancestors count more enemies

than friends of Rome. So I smiled
at each shrivelled corpse we defiled,
repurposed for our new foundations
as backfill. Our empire was to come –

a Gallic empire. I was here to learn
only the mechanics of obliteration.
I stacked their bricks with hate, disdain.
Rome could shrink like a dried-up stain.

Both/Neither

Inscribed grave goods, Southwark, London, 65 CE

Unexpectedly a DNA analysis identified male chromosomes....

For years I'd strayed between borders, fallen
in the cracks. I read Latin. I spoke British.
I dressed for the hunt as well as the forum.
My hands were stained with blood. And rouge.

Then late one night at a flickering taper
I was transformed by the lines of a poet:
no longer man nor woman but both, neither...
This Ovid burned for me, my own prophet

who knew my life, my faith. My difference.
I picked a path through sleeping streets,
the fog lifting and the sleet just cleared
as Orion split the sky into wavering stars –

a time caught between autumn and winter.
I'd seen subjection, revolt, reconstruction.
Now their forums shivered in recognition.
By the temples, I'd taste ice-tinged kisses

fierce, fleeting, first snow on my parched lips.
I'd track another skin in new-found worship.
As my due, I would claim the city's praises,
demand respect without apology or remorse.

And when I left, far too soon, they might weep,
offer wine for my journey, the comfort of meats;
a Vitalis bowl to cup my life, a feathered torque
for the goddess I had to worship, always would.

A bronze mirror to keep my reflection safe,
its secret, as I'd prayed, unguessed, unknown.
That traitor code it would take millennia to break.
The when – and Y – seared through my bones.

By Bread and Salt

Writing tablet, Walbrook, London, 66 CE

By bread and salt, please repay promptly
all you owe in silver change, 26 denarii…

We found the note among his things
(I doubt he'd settled up, knowing him).

By bread and salt… I was a child again
sniggering at his old-fashioned sayings:

chant three times to cure your fever
he'd insist at the end of our sick-beds

as he grinned and tipped his head,
looking at the world through a crack

no one else could find. Stormy days
were *a bit grey over Aufer's mother's.*

When we fidgeted, kept in by the gales:
oh well, it's a sunny day in Dacia…

And as the downpours started to clear,
look: enough blue for a Pict's jockstrap –

our favourite which had us in guffaws.
We were too small, didn't understand

but still we laughed just the same.
He promised he would never leave us.

Then one morning he slipped away.
All we had left was the sound of rain.

To Mogontius in London...

Inscribed clay dice, Malton, North Yorkshire &
Writing tablet, Walbrook, London 67 CE.

I remember how they weighted
down your hands as if hard lead
not clay; how you kissed the die
before it fell, a wind-caught sigh:

It's decided. I go to the city.
I was left to balance the risks.
You wrote of ever-stacking roofs
stretched across the city skies

like grass rippling on our heaths.
And, as always, one last throw,
the unchallenged rule of chance:
Join me here. Bring the kids.

I wanted to see it, this new life.
To understand what you built,
tile by brittle tile, brick by brick.
The sun-baked blocks. The heat.

Every day I mould another street...
Beyond the village, the autumn
light smouldered through the moors.
By the fires some still talked of war.

I watched the scribe struggle
with his long, steep stroke of 'L',
marring his mark, letting stylus drift.
I felt the deep wax part and shift

as it hardened into capital: *London.*
The sharp drop of a heart turned
over. A sudden wake from sleep.
The dots jolted as they land.

That freefall, lurching pull of home.

Will

Writing tablet, Walbrook, London, 68 CE

I [insert name here] of the Vangion
First Cohort bequeath to my son:

The cries of butchers in the market halls,
haze of blacksmiths, hum of metalworkers;
a scent of spice from across the empire,
stench of piss trickling out from tanners' stalls.

The swell of every language: Gallic, Greek,
German, Numidian, Thracian, Phrygian.
The swagger of swollen businessmen
claiming their ownership of our coined streets.

The shade of gardens and hidden courtyards.
A breath-held stillness in the morning bars
as lonely veterans drain one last beer
by the bones of their half-built arena.

This brutal, brimful, unpredictable
city. The air we built it from. The will.

Thief

Writing tablet, Walbrook, London, 69 CE

for Attius the thief, at Rochester...

I knew it the first day I saw him.

A chill November morning, the sun
sharpening the room we'd stumbled
back to the night before; his small bed
at one end, a shelf for cracked Samian,
worn chair piled with clothes. The way
he peeled the stiff tunic from my body
murmuring my name as if it was his
to take. A sacred enchantment. A curse.
As if he'd always believed I'd come.
A client. In his debt. *Marcus. Marcus.*

Yes, I knew it. All was over. Lost.

Outside, the world spun. Emperors
changed by the hour. Our governors
fled. Now time was a breath suspended
between the dawn cries of forum traders
and rhythmic chants of recalled soldiers
falling away as the day scuttled to its end.
On the roof the tiles hissed with rain
while we made love over and over again.

Then one morning he said he was leaving.
Out in the market it was trying to snow.
Our sanctuary, too, had ice in the air:
he talked of Rochester, a new legion.
Rochester. The name was like poison.
I lay in bed all day trying to read, alone:
Ovid, Catullus, the passion of *Myrmidons*:
my love remember the nights we shared...
I saw his eyes, flecked with fiery topaz,

inhaled the scent of his hop-soaked skin.
Through the walls, someone coughed
or shuffled across the creaky floor above.
I read on. The city was empty. A husk.

Attius, you thief, come back to London.
Return it to me, the heart you have stolen.

Keepsake
Inscribed writing stylus, Walbrook, London, 75 CE

From Rome, a keepsake to bring you pleasure –
a pointed gift so you will always remember;
I wish I could have given you much, much more
but the journey is long and funds are short.

I'm sure he threw it in the stream. London,
I'd heard, was in ferment, packed with pleasure:
fine wines, sweet ale, and most of all women,
its frost-edged dusk a lure to warm the bones.

My message, sharpened, in miniature,
would go unread, unmarked. He didn't know
there was a further present still to come
from that brief, jasmined night he'd forgotten –
those pared hours we shared before he embarked –

but I relived by day; how the moon grazed
the sea at Ostia like a polished blade
as each serrated kiss cut time in half.

A keepsake to bring you pleasure. Ten days
old. Her father in replica. As sharp.

The House Opposite
Writing tablet, Walbrook, London, 80 CE

Give this note to the cooper Junius,
just opposite the house of Catullus...

I unpack my treasures of Syrian glass,
plates sourced from the slopes of Vesuvius.
The walls I paint with frail shoots of grass
and a poppy – my own hidden message
for those who know the poet, my namesake:
a flower fallen at the meadow's edge...

I had pictured myself as a pioneer
composing dark, difficult northern poems
as fêted (one day) as my famed forebear.
Besides I'd been priced out of Rome.

Yet each word I write I later delete.

I watch the starlings rising up at dusk
above the teeming, cloud-fogged streets
like a simile slipping out of grasp.
I hear the drunken Rhenish equites
chant their alehouse verse, swilled in vomit –
our bleak reward for seven months' back pay.
My voice is clogged with London clay.

All I am here is the house opposite
the cooper, two doors down from the brewer.
The only lines that come, come in error
and for them: barrels, bills, more calls for beer.

Catullus the Slave

Writing tablet, Walbrook, London, 80 CE

To Catullus the slave of Romanius Faustinus:
2000 units, 65 denarii [lines struck through]

Nine months on, the cold kicked in.
My page was sleet white, its lines
still frozen. By the following year
I had given up, sold everything –

volcanic crockery to the cooper,
ink-smudged glass to the brewer
who was branching out to wine.
When even that was not enough

I sold myself to Romanius Faustinus,
a scrawny Gallic works contractor
(a literary man, he said, was worth
more than most). I did his books.

I counted bricks, tessera for mosaics
shifting back into the face of Orpheus,
accounts closed, nothing outstanding.
I learnt silence where once I spoke –

he owned the air, he owned my breath –
so I mouthed the verse I used to quote,
the finest Catullus (snr) had written:
you pea-brain, hairy-legged hick

whose farts are your best feature...
And concurred re bastard Caesar:
why did he ever eye up Britain
that cursed place, ugly and remote?

Account

Writing tablet, Walbrook, London, 82 CE

Supplied to Crispus's tavern:
Beer, 5 denarii [1000 pints]
*   7 denarii [1400 pints]*

Night after night we had the thankless task
of keeping the city watered. As soon
as one emptied we'd fill another cask
until our streets brimmed with swaying legions
waiting on their orders (by all reports
our rash new governor, that ambitious
arsewipe Agricola, would now march north).

I didn't blame them. As a veteran
I knew those roads, the rigid, bone-strewn paths
that level worlds while names, careers, are built.
This was Caledonia: dark, unmapped,
uncrossed, its tarns as deep as hidden guilt,
its forests trembling like a long-planned trap.

Every drop they drained would soon be spilt.

Too Far

Grampian Mountains, Scotland, 83 CE

…through the waging of war Agricola found respite from his sorrow…

I tried to describe how it had felt – the furthest
any Roman had ever come. That overcast August
day in Caledonia I buried a son. Troops massed

against us, countless on the blotted mountains.
But I would never turn back to mourn him.
I went out to battle, to breed my same grief:

they create a wasteland and call it peace…
Afterwards I walked in the northern forests;
an unearthly twilight seeped on past sunset

through hacked limbs, the mounds of the fallen,
its skies steeped in their blood like a sponge.
I had stepped over the edge of the known

world and was standing in the meadows
of fading stars, on grass flayed by the breeze,
caught in the nets of skeletal wildflower seed.

Clouds spiralled above, shattered sphincters,
linking us together, conquered and conqueror.
Too far. The furthest anyone had ever come.

The living and the dead in a moth's wingspan.
I knew that this soil could never be cleansed.
Even in Hades, we would not see our sons again.

The Cavalry
Writing tablet, Walbrook, London, 84 CE

[*insert name here*] *received a loan*

Witnessed by:
Longinus, troop of Marinus
Agrippa, troop of Silvanus
Verecundus, troop of Silvanus

We're the lucky ones who made it back
unscathed, still able to give a signature
and remember (just) who we once were:

Longinus had wanted to open a smithy
but could no longer keep his hand steady.
Agrippa fancied leather or metal-working

but cowered at any sudden flash or bang.
I, Verecundus, dreamt of marriage, a son.
But what woman on earth would put up

with a temper that was no longer my own?
We knew we could not forget Caledonia
yet all of us were agreed: we would never

speak of it again. Once we were The Cavalry.
Now we bear witness only to those in need
of a hand, a loan. Our price for getting home.

The Case of the Missing Mules
Writing tablet, Walbrook, London, 90 CE

…Catarrius came and stole them,
the master's beasts of burden…

I wish I had never taken the brief
or ever heard of those dratted donkeys.

To recap. They belonged to Macrinus
but Taurus (or Taurinus?) his lackey
had the job of transporting them from whence
to Jove knows where when one Catarrius –
the nose wipe – snaffled them, it seems, by stealth,
while Taurus, Jove knows why, was away, safe
with Diadumenus for a night only…

Confused? Believe me, I've hardly started.
Now Taurus swears he can't make recompense
for the missing mules, not in three harvests.

So here's the burning question we should ask:
does London really need another ass?

Coinage

Writing tablet, Walbrook, London, 95 CE

From Rufus to Epillicus The Steward,
*   At My London House*
Write the list. See that you work through
it carefully. Ensure you cash in the due
value of the girl and sell her as directed.
Make hard coin out of soft flesh…

These days I don't remember Nubia,
a shadow shrinking in some distant room.

In London I'm part of the inventory.
Rufus, my trader, fusses with his lists –
acquired himself, he craves acquisition.
I watch the hands of his new auditors
as they move like lovers on abacus
and tally, caressing stone currency.

At the docks I search out fresh-landed ships
whose crews might share my face. I follow them
upstream, entranced by language, a coinage
to chime in my blood if not on my lips.
On the shore I step in sodden footprints
as if that speech might ooze up from the silt.

To Rufus, I'm spare change, mere leverage.
One day here I will broker my own voice.

II.

Through Clay

*… you can bridge chasms of time and space simply by walking
from one room to the next…*
        (Killian Fox, *Are ghosts haunting the British
        Museum?, The Economist,* 28th April, 2020)

At the Temple of Isis

Inscribed clay jug, Southwark, London, 90 CE

We meet to drink and to remember Egypt.

We talk of the journey west, how our ship
docked first at Delos: 'Welcome to Greece'
the crew said. And I wept, an Alexandrian
who knew she had come home. At Emporion
the sand was as unsullied as our priests'
lustral robes, its sea a gold-streaked lapis.

But we left Spain for this filthy, sluggish
northern river. We enthroned our goddess
by its tainted banks, carving out cisterns
to decant foul waters into pure white flagons.

On street corners we chant transgressions.
Our neighbours avoid us. No one listens.
As dusk falls we wait for waking visions –
one day, in dreams, She will find Her way.
We pray, we sing, we celebrate Her feasts.
This city thrums with rhythms of the east.

In London at the Temple of Isis…
We will impress our faith through its soft clay.

In Athens

Tombstone, Tower Hill, London, 100 CE

He said they were the most exquisite words
in any language. I can see him on the quay
bowing as he introduced himself, undeterred,
as if he knew, despite his age, such beauty
and grace would have us instantly enthralled.

It's true: his eyes were still a deep cerulean,
his smile calmed like a ship reaching landfall,
his face was a monument, one of the ancients.
Still he carried with him a trace of the Aegean
if he now spoke Greek with a slight Latin accent.

Aulus Alfidius Olussa. Even etched on a tomb
his name was an involuntary sigh. Or a poem
almost-made, nearing completion. Yet between
'70 years' and 'here lies' there was some room,
enough – surely just enough – to squeeze it in.
The only epitaph he required: *Born in Athens.*

Cure-All
Oculist's stamps, Upper Thames Street, London, 120 CE

Gaius Silvius Tetricus's cure-all miced from diamisus
Medicinal misy for scars of the eye, any cicatrix

Gaius Silvius Tetricus's double-use biprosopum
For an attack or sudden onset of blurred vision

Gaius Silvius Tetricus's ointment for the onset
Of rheum and blurred vision, blearedness

Made by hand from finest fragrant euodes
Gaius Silvius Tetricus's scented draught for eye lids

We had smiled at his Gallic Greek ('Grallic'
you'd called it): *euodes* or 'cloying draught',
diamisus which meant a 'bitter taste'

and double-use *biprosopum* ('two-faced') –
a salve that came in drops or ointment stick
(double the disgust, we might once have laughed).

Today I watch you creep to the river
passing on nostrums like an infection
to whichever girl you have installed there.
A sudden attack of blurred vision…
and your wife of twelve years invisible.

Bitter taste. Two-faced. A so-called cure-all.
I count my coins. I need a remedy
to make you see better. Make you see me.

Catullus's Barrel
Supplier's stamp, Cheapside, London 135 CE

```
        Q
        V
        E
        T
    QVETCATUL
        A
        T
        U
        L
```

Quintus Vettius Catullus

Once we were intoxicated by words
my father told me, a family of poets;

we metered out desire, or anguish,
heady proof, as our meanings slurred.

But verse costs. Ditto fine luxury.
Soon he'd been in debt, in slavery.

He bought himself back, a new career –
where the money lay, he said. In beer.

I followed him. For these long decades
my name has been stamped on barrels

yet I'm a stranger to myself. I line capitals,
tilting letters as they interlock, cascade,

trying to connect who I am, what I make.
Tonight, as I watch from our dank hold,

a confusion of sparrows, drunk on space
and light, suddenly disrupts, dissipates

across blank February skies then flows
back into form and shape as if syllable

on syllable, a forfeited poem pulled
from cloud and air. Below, under a pile

of crumpled bills and unmatched receipts,
I find my father's desk, its wax and pots.

I soak his stylus slowly, take the ink neat.
I will reel, I know, from its first drop.

Seafarer

Marble slab, Tabard Street, South London, 161 CE

*To the Divine Emperors and Mars Camulus
Tiberinius Celerianus of the Bellovaci, Moritix,
Seafarer, the first Londoner to… [dedicates this]*

They say that you always know the start
if not the end. I must have made a thousand
crossings, turbulent in our skiffs. On the first,
I remember, I was so sick the captain laughed.
Mid-sea, we were suddenly suffocated by fog.
We slowed to stillness. Time itself had stopped.
I could hear cries from unseen crafts like ghosts
trapped in their waterlogged worlds, warning us
to keep, to stay away. Suddenly we saw land,
cliffs through a cleft in the clouds. My captain
patted me on the back. Baptism, he said, by mist.

Now I am a captain myself, rank of *Moritix*:
Cross-Channel Seafarer, the first Londoner to.
Still I fear those freighted, moon-dragged
waters. I pray for protection to my own god,
Mars Camulus – and to the emperors, in lieu.
The first Londoner to…. The first… The first.

I make these offerings so I won't be the last.

God Help Demetrios

Pewter amulet, Upper Thames Street, London,169 CE

friendly gods,
divinites, whirl
away all heart-
pounding, ear-
shrieking, breath-
piercing, air-
carrying plague;

spare us its men-
destroying, skin-
penetrating, spirit-
weighting, flesh-
devouring, bone-
dissolving, vein-
hollowing pain….

God help
Demetrios

When the Watch turned him over he was rashed,
mottled with sores. The same plague (and fifth corpse)
we'd seen that day, each clutching amulets
for 'protection'. Their Greek was chalked on doors
to stem pestilence with prayer, gibberish –
the pus-filled promise of charlatans' charms.
And yet those same houses reeked most of death
as if enchantments inflamed infection.

Demetrios fed our pits. His talisman
we tipped in the Thames. Maybe it cost him
but the pewter was not worth salvaging
for fear of fresh taint, contamination.

All hearts stopped as he twitched. We'd been disarmed.
And we'd been wrong: poetry might save one.

The Most Devoted

Inscription, Moorgate, London, 170 CE

Her Latin was imperfect – they were Greeks –
but she insisted on the word just so
(all else, bar their given names, was in brief).
And I complied: FIL • PIENTISSIMO
the most devoted son, picked out in red.

She had chosen our standard 'compact square'
(if imported stone, the most expensive)
as her squeezed signature • *EUCARPIA* •
grazed the end like a shrivelled codicil.

Still she wanted to total his full sum:
YE[ARS] • FIFTEEN • M[ONTHS] • SIX
for those he'd had rather than those he'd miss,
that half-time, half-life, to which she clung: FIL •
PIENTISSIMO • *most devoted son*.

Bricking It

Clay tile with graffito, Newgate Street, London, 185 CE

Today, and every day for the last thirteen,
Austalis is skiving, is nowhere to be seen

It was never meant to be malicious.

We all scratched names to bond the fix.
Or maybe to retain a little of ourselves
as those vast, defensive walls were built.

But for weeks he had been playing us.
He'd vanish like kiln smoke to return,
half-plastered, from Crispus's tavern,
insistent he'd been on urgent business
though we knew he was barely literate –
faced with letters he'd be bricking it.

So we laid a trap, played our own joke.
I wrote the lines, no more than doggerel
from a song I'd heard in the brothels,
fractured Latin but the way we spoke.

Later, after the clay had hardened,
I propped it up on the brickwork gates:
a monument to this mercurial town
of cheats, malingerers and reprobates.

And the way words, too, solidify, set
into blocks, bonded, one by one, piece
by piece – the only one in the only
place – strengthening into lines, leaf
slotted on leaf, on and on, recut
into houses, streets, shifting cities;

how, when these walls are levelled,
our names, our jokes, will be left
still scrawled across in crude relief.

Celsus the Spy
Inscription, Blackfriars, London, 195 CE

With offerings to the spirits of the dead,
here lies Celsus, son of Lucius, a Claudian,
speculator of the Augusta Second Legion:
Dardanus, Valerius Pudens and Probus,
his fellow scouts, set this stone up…

I kept my ear to the ground and my eye
on the gutter. From below, our world
glowed in sewers, grease-swirled gullies
like soiled, discoloured mother-of-pearl.
The wife scolded I stayed out all hours
rolling home sober with a broken nose –
another stop and search turned sour.

In Britain, there were just the four of us:
Dardanus, Valerius, Probus and myself
('spy' is an ugly word, as is 'executioner'
we prefer 'scout', in Latin *speculator*).
Just four of us who knew, who understood
what it's like to live outside, beyond truth.
Even our old legion, we've heard, is split;
when your own allegiance is fracturing
it's hard to know who – or what – to spy on.

Shuddering awake, I think of throats I've slit
in the dark, the stuttering groan of the knife
as skin softly rips and blood drips through
the stemmed drains, a bile-drenched dew.

Whatever happens the lads will see me right.

Thumbs Up

Gladiator grave lamps, Southwark, London, 220 CE

*One further factor needs to be taken into account…this was
the grave of a woman…*

Even as a girl I was besotted, mesmerised.
For my tenth birthday my father sent me
to the Games. He told me we were Isaics,
Syrians, who honoured the boundaries

between passing worlds, this and the next.
We did not come, he warned, to watch men die
but to rehearse our own, approaching deaths.
I learnt that we all stare through the cracks

of the Underworld. Gladiators report back.
That day I understood how it feels to breathe
by common lungs; how our fear pulses
through a shared vein, a spider's thread spun

across from warrior to warrior to spectator.
Time passed. Once, somewhere, I gave birth;
my first kill was on account. The rest
without remorse. Thrust by thrust, lunge

by lunge, roar by roar, I matched the men
in battle lust. Now my own death is here.
I light its rusted path with lamps for Anubis
keeper of secrets, weigher of souls. I wait

at his trembling threshold to beg for *missio*
and redemption. Thumbs up. As I hesitate
in that closing light, I hear the hushed slow
hum of blood. And then walk with courage

from arena into gore-sluiced darkness.

Hector's

Inscribed child's leather sole, Walbrook, London, 290 CE

Now, suddenly, he was wearing shoes.

I remember that first pair. He was four
and, mimicking his namesake, waging war,
one-to-one combat in the race to lose.
He'd hurl them off while I cajoled, coaxed,
as if struggling to shed that part of him
I had dressed, had turned out, before hobbling
home defiant, swerving my hand. I wrote
his name in Greek on the sole – precaution,
yes, but now, as he ran, he'd stamp himself
like a scribe on the city's sludge and silt.

One kick by the stream and the shoe was gone.

My legion moved on. I went home to Asia,
Ilium. His mother stopped writing. Each year
I swore I would go back. I never did.
By now he'd be married, maybe kids
who might drop their own shoes at the river.

Somewhere in those sky-crushed October streets
his name lingers like a relic, a leaf
pressed between wind-rattled stones, still caught there.
The leavings of our dust-sketched prints: *Hector's*.

In Pieces
Tomb of Julius Classicianus, Tower Hill, London, 375 CE

When Felix found the slabs, problem solved.
We all sighed in relief. They'd plug the hole.

Until his men turned them over to reveal it:
CLASSICIANI • PROC • PROVINC • BRIT
Classicianus, Procurator, Province of Britain.
I looked at Felix then back at the inscription.
He bit his lip. If we didn't shore up the wall
none of us would get paid. It was my call.

By the tower, the spring tide ebbed, silting.
The river shrank like an unhealed lesion.
I brushed that broken lettering: *IULIA • UXOR •*
Yet we too had wives, families to support.
And now our own world was starting to crack.
We had the pieces but could not fit them back.

I'd heard enough. We dug the ditch. We made the fill.
No one spoke. No one saw. I doubt they ever will.

After the Flood
Pelagian tracts, London, 411 CE

Don't believe what they wrote or what they said –
some of us rejoiced when the legions left.
You think that the world is falling apart,
we sneered. *So what? This is only the start.*
Yes, after the flood men were more devout.

We had heard how London was in revolt
and saw our chance: *we can, we will, we are.*
Root out the rich and there will be no poor.

We were dreamers, heretics: Pelagians.
We had to act where we found oppression.
We lived only by righteousness. God's Law.
To the pure, we agreed, *all things are pure.*
Man could – and would – do always what is right.

But no one gives up wealth without a fight.

Purged streets were polluted, sullied by blood,
bodies left unburied, flesh for carrion.
Those who had been our judges we now judged.
We changed wives to widows, child to orphan.

To the pure all things are… After the flood
we had overlooked, we had forgotten
one truth: what Briton will do to Briton.

Dark Earth

London, 420 CE

And then we lived like ghosts in our cities.

Decay crept outwards from centre to edge
but we held firm, jeering at those who fled.
Markets crashed so we buried our money.
Sickness shadowed us on the streets. We stayed
at home. In time we knew nothing of towns
beyond our own. Squares, gardens, all spare land
we turned to crops. Fights were stopped, games not played.
In the arena baiting bears ran free.

We are sinking back into History,
dark earth, the detritus of worn empires.
All we are. All we've been. All that matters.

We sow words in wood, through clay, on stone walls.
We know if we stay silent, darkness falls.

For Evalus, Son of

Inscribed stone, Spittal church porch, West Wales, 520 CE

I chose the largest slab we could haul.

We needed the space for its capitals,
lettered down, right to left, in verticals.
I remember watching the new cutter
tracing each one slowly with his hands,
squinting at my script, a bleared picture
of some far, other world, just ended,
symbols he could no longer understand.

As he chiselled, I felt the granite chips fall
like our sudden squalls of autumn rain.
I saw him smooth down the near edge
patting it softly as if putting a child to bed.
And there it was. A dedication. A name:
For Evalus, son of. With mine: *Cuniovende.*

I had thought we would be the last
who could – or want – to read that Latin.
Yet heads have tilted for a millennium
and a half, like birds, as they passed:
the neat assistant from the corner shop
in her pleated skirts and curled-up hair
counting kids in and out. Except her own.
The schoolmistress shushing her class
into all but one of its shrunken chairs.
Each maid who slipped their kitchen lock
to drop blood-soaked parcels at the lych-gate.
The shunned, the silent, the toppled saints.

Every Sunday for fifteen hundred years
they have paused by us in this place

and mouthed our grassy, guilt-gnawed words
to make them true: *Mater Eius. His mother.*
To keep them near. To keep them safe.

Ghost Passage
Kent, 553 CE

(after Procopius)

Late at night, they hear banging at their doors,
a voice, indistinct, calling them to task.
They do not shrink. They wake, walk to the shore
confused by their compulsion, or who asks,
compelled to act just the same. They find boats
like their own if not quite. Somehow other.

As they lift out the oars they feel the load
like lead ballast, a haul of passengers.
They see soaked planks lying low in the depths
of the waters, lapped to the very edge
of the rowlocks – barely a finger's breadth
above the surge – but no more, no one else.

Within a long hour they return to Kent,
Thanatos, isle of the dead. That tare weight
lifts. They hear nothing, no steps disembark
yet the same voice urges them to take charge
of these lost souls: all the ghosts of France, Spain,
Italy – and Britain. As each descends
their achievements are called in requiem.
Their kindness. Their partners, their parents' names.
Those they had loved. All those who had loved them.

III.

On Stone (Oxney sonnets)

Not many folk of substance and standing have resided in the village…

(W.H. Yeandle, *Historical Notes on the Church of Stone-in-Oxney. Kent,* 1993)

i.

Bull
Roman altar stone, Stone-in-Oxney church

Once I was led through the streets garlanded
with flowers and rare jewels. Kings paid homage.
Philosophers shook at my touch. They said
that when I died, priests and seers shaved their heads
while stern dictators wept. I was their god
and their pet: Apis, Lord of Life. And Loss.

I prefer it here. That homesick sailor,
shivering for the heat of Alexandria,
who carved your rough Kent sandstone, set me free.
Now I am always mid-leap. Mugs of tea
warm my flanks. Stacked sheaves of parish minutes
serve as diadems for my head. I finish
your devotions, sing hymns with my dust breath.

I run with you into each mildewed death.

ii

White
Isle of Oxney, Kent, May, 991

....this place also was by the Danes piteously spoiled and burnt...

After London, Oxney seemed so easy.

We slid through its streams by a marauders'
moon, a milk moon, to guide us in the dusk.
Everywhere blazed white – daisies, cow parsley,
horse chestnut candles – as if we had slipped
back in time to face a fierce new winter.
Above us, a penitent patch lingered
on the slopes; hawthorn drifted round its cliffs
like a late, phantom fall across the Marsh.

We pressed on. To us their timber houses,
each precious church, were no more than kindling
for our ice fires. And we prefer blood-red;
the only white we might want to see is
flickering, pure. At the edge of a flame.

iii

Shadowtime
Winchelsea, 1287

That night a slice of moon rose, mottled red
like a scratched wound. The sea was torched, wind-charged.
We heard the tide roar twice across the Marsh
and knew it was here, the hour of the dead.

Hulls creaked. Roofs lifted. Churches sunk. Great oaks
were wrenched from roots. Rivers swelled in ferment
until they became our streets. While we dreamt
the earth shifted in shadowtime. We woke

to find oceans where we'd once farmed. Islands
landlocked, hamlets now great ports. And our town
lost to us, buried like some secret shame
beneath a crookbacked bank of bone-packed sand.

From beneath, I smooth your prints, pay the debt.
And I whisper. I warn you. Watch. Your. Step.

Block
The Vicarage, Stone-in-Oxney, 1716

Rev. Culpepper Savage would not be mocked.

As soon as his sextons had unearthed it –
Relique of Heathenisims, sacrilege –
they dragged the slab outside as jossing block,
there to be stamped by boot and smeared in dung;
an altar to gods no sane man worshipped,
false idols for pagans who had cursed it –
a rampant bull in charge, flanked by oxen.

Harsh winters wore away the craven beasts.
When the Reverend tried to mount his mare
all footings slipped. Stone cracked in summer heat.
The block shuddered. Sometimes it moved (some swore).
Its bull seemed to rear. Sorcery. Witchcraft.

Yet again his horse threw him on his arse.

Left Side Blank

Stone-in-Oxney churchyard

Richard Bathhurst May ye 5 1727 age 39

I can see him in those Sunday parlours,
double-dusted, stiff with expectation,
bewildered by giggling farmer's daughters
with no clue what he might say to women.

When he'd turned one and thirty the headstones
were his birthday gift. Precaution, prudence,
his father said. Priced fair by the masons –
a skull for him, an hour glass for his spouse.

Maybe, once, he found someone who was kind,
older, just losing hope of child or house;
who might promise one bud-shot May to wait,
to join him (there would always be a space).

From time to time he turns and reaches out.
It still feels so cold on the other side.

vi

Bedded In
Player family grave, Stone-in-Oxney churchyard, 1840–1895

They have made their own king-size, child-safe bed
and now lie in it; linked stones at the feet
for stubbed toes and another two for heads
topped with downy feather, pillowed by seed
and elder, milk-parsley, speedwell. Curled in
beneath, Harriet (died eighteen sixty-three,
aged forty-five) crooks a child in each arm –
maybe her namesake, still just a baby,
or Edwin who could count his years to five –
drawing off tears with the same distractions:
the sluice of drains where snipe or lapwings dive,
a daisy-chain of lanes, the blurred ferry
just crossed. And far above, a grey heron
rising like a smear on the horizon.

vii

Jazz

Stone-in-Oxney churchyard

Giuseppina
Nov. 6ᵗʰ 1914–19ᵗʰ May 1915

Look for my bugle-bound, three-quarter grave,
a breath-stop life. The four beat name we share
picked out in lead Grotesk: GIUSEPINNA.
I still keep time here, November to May,
as spring blossom's blown, chestnut candles damped
back down. FOR SUCH IS THE KINGDOM OF GOD…

In my six months I knew only war – Ypres,
Gallipoli – as I slept in my crib
dreaming of a great age. But that spring night
in Chicago, Tom Brown's Dixieland Band
first syncopated drums for their new sound,
too late for me, I faded from the fight.

I miss those note-pierced hours I never had.
Dancing. Laughter. Ragtime for ragwort. Jazz.

A Few Feet
Old Romney churchyard

A shorn-off column marks the breaths not spent
of *Joseph Reginald Herbert Cooper*
who *fell ill while serving his country…* Spring
nineteen-nineteen, the war six months over.
Aged Nineteen. Still it managed to claim him.
Beside him a burrow bound with green wire fence
holds *Sergeant W. J. Stephen, Air Gunner.*
Nineteen forty-four. Once again *Nineteen.*

As in the mess, they stretch out, ankles crossed,
arms behind heads, exchanging fags, pictures
of sweethearts and blotted, thumb-marked letters.
Or plan that swift one in The Rose & Crown
while words hang like stopped dandelion clocks

and the next war waits, just a few feet on.

ix

In Infancy
Stone-in-Oxney & Wittersham churchyards

Beyond the stark, beige Commission headstones
and buffed bronze tablets nailed to chancel arch
there is another conflict, a war zone
whose numbers are unknown. Or worse, unasked:

two stillborn sons… George 10 October died
on the same day… 4 daughters in one grave…
Ann in ye 6th year… William born July
died July… John 6 months, Stephen 4 days…

Too many here to register, to count:
entrenched, relentless lines of casualties
winding round like ivy until stones tilt
and names are spent, bullet-holed – an assault
not just on childhood but *in infancy*.
This roll of poverty and class and want.

X

Visitors' Book
Snargate church

(*i.m. Darlene Balmer*)

Turning its pages, crinkled as damp skin,
we find her handwriting like an old friend
strangely met, out of context: *10/10/10.*
A day she's marked to perfection, looping
the joint '*D*'s in her name and my title,
still new then, even here the proud mother.
I reach down to release her snagged pleasure
to skim her soft, cupped hand: *So beautiful…*

…mould, plaster, *L'Air du Temps*, inhaled again,
the Doom Boards read aloud, the wall-daubed ship
nearly-sailed. Less than six weeks left with her
before our dates, our lines, will be taken
by these others, thickened with different scripts:
pilgrims, walkers, ancestor worshippers.

Half-Size

Girl's jewellery, Museum of London, present day

(for Rachel and Tre)

More than twenty years on and the old wound
still reopens. Among the uncast die
and never-cashed chips of dimmed Roman rooms,
a cache of semi-precious stones, half-size,
breath-frail, for a girl of maybe seven
or eight – the grave, unfastened offerings
of another family now, too, gone:
the hollows of bracelets, her tiny ring
poised above like a miniature halo;
an unclasped thread of pearls, scarred amethysts
aching for the frame of her eager face.

I know each heart-stab gap. I nod hello
as if to lapsed acquaintance: this homeless
restless love that waits like an unfilled space.

Historical Sources and Notes

Poems based on the Bloomberg writing tablets were inspired by the cache of tablets found during excavations at the Bloomberg London Building, 2010–14. I am indebted to Roger Tomlin for his decipherment and edited commentary, *Roman London's first voices: Writing Tablets from the Bloomberg excavation, 2010–14* (MOLA, 2016). All Bloomberg tablets are annotated WT followed by their edition number.

RIB = *The Roman Inscriptions of Britain Vols I–III* (Alan Sutton/Oxbow, 1965–2009).

Apart from a few dated writing tablets and known historical events, dates given for the poems are estimations, based on archaeological reports.

WRITER[?], LONDON
(for Charlotte Parkyn)
Bloomberg WT 18 contains the Latin word '*Londinio*' and possibly also *scriba*, a secretary or writer, the first recorded mention of the profession in London, although the word appears to have been scratched through as if written in error. The poem also quotes WT 55, a loan note.

frail: a leaf skeleton where only the vein network remains (Robert Macfarlane, *Landmarks*, Hamish Hamilton, 2015, p.309).

I. IN WOOD

CICERO (MINOR) CONQUERS BRITAIN
Head quote from Cicero, *Letters to His Brother Quintus*, 3.1.
Quintus Tullius Cicero was four years younger than his more famous brother Marcus, the Roman statesman and orator. Quintus served with Julius Caesar in Britain, a post to which several of Marcus's letters refer. He shared Marcus's literary ambitions, particularly as a tragedian, but never matched his brother's success. Almost all of his works are now lost. With Marcus, Quintus was proscribed after the assassination of Caesar and executed in 43 BCE.

THE FIRST EUROPEAN
The tombstone of the Thracian cavalryman, Longinus Sdapeze, was found in Colchester in 1928 (RIB. 201). Its early date, just a few years

after Claudius's invasion in 43 CE, suggests Longinus was one of the emperor's own troops. It tells us that he was of the rank of *duplicarius* which meant he received twice the basic rate of pay. The tombstone is now on display in the Colchester Castle Museum.

Agassia: As well as oysters and wool, Britain was famous for its Agassian breed of hunting dogs.

PECKING ORDERS
Bloomberg WT 30, is probably the first financial document recorded in the City of London, and offers proof of economic activity in the early years of Roman London. It was sent to one Titus Aviarius or 'Titus Birdkeeper', and appears to be a sneer by the unnamed writer against his fellow, less experienced businessman, perhaps a new arrival in the city.

IN THE SECOND CONSULSHIP OF NERO
Bloomberg WT 44, a loan document, is the earliest dated tablet from Roman London. Venustus, the name of the freedman Tibullus's ex-master, also occurs in WT 45 (see 'Provisions') although it is not clear if this is the same man. Tibullus is also the name of a Roman elegiac poet (55 BCE–19 CE).

Nero will abolish all taxes: According to Tacitus (*Annals*, 13.50), Nero's promise was abandoned after the Senate pointed out that 'the empire would die without its revenue'.

DESTRUCTION HORIZON
Head quote from Tacitus, *Annals*, 14.33.
In archaeology a destruction horizon is a layer of earth containing ash, soot and burnt artefacts denoting a past catastrophic event. During Boudica's revolt in 61 CE, Suetonius Paulinus, the governor of Britain, decided to abandon London, although he later defeated the rebellious British tribes to the north of the city. The horizon left by Boudica's subsequent sack of London is still apparent in the city's archaeology. The poem draws on the accounts of Tacitus and Dio Cassius (*Histories*, 62.1), particularly the omens that presaged Boudica's destruction of the city.

NEW ROMAN
Bloomberg WT 79 is scored simply with letters of the Roman alphabet, possibly used for teaching literacy. Its early date suggests that London

recovered swiftly from Boudica's revolt.

ENUMERATION
Bloomberg WT 78 contains numbers and Roman numerical symbols, probably for trading accounts.

PROVISIONS
Bloomberg WT 45, an agreement to transport grain from St Albans to London, is precisely dated to 21 October 62 CE, a few years after the destruction of both cities during Boudica's revolt. It illustrates how they must have been rebuilt far more quickly than previously thought. The name Venustus also appears in WT 44 (see 'In the Second Consulship of Nero').

elbow's length: The text of the tablet appears to mention *ulnam omnem* or 'whole elbow' which might refer to a measurement – or a penalty.

BACKFILL
Bloomberg WT 33 mentions the Gallo-Roman nobleman Julius Classicus, later infamous as one of the leaders of a Gallic uprising against Rome at Cologne in 69/70 CE. His presence in Britain was previously unknown. He might have been related to Julius Classicianus, the governor of Britain credited with rebuilding London after Boudica's revolt (see 'In Pieces').

as if enjoying the fruits…: Based on Tacitus, *Histories*, 4.70.

BOTH/NEITHER
Head quote from 'Written in Bone: New Discoveries about the Lives and Burials of Four Roman Londoners', Rebecca Redfern et al, *Britannia* 48 (November 2017), 253–77.
Originally excavated in 1979, the grave's bones were deemed to be female. A later DNA test by the Museum of London in 2015 for its 'Written in Bone' exhibition revealed male chromosomes (XY) although the grave goods suggest its occupant was identified by her community as a woman. These include a bowl marked with its maker's stamp, *Vitalis*, possibly chosen for its Latin pun on 'of life', a torque whose peacock-feather pattern could refer to Juno, the Roman goddess of female fertility and childbirth, and a rare bronze mirror. Analysis showed the occupant of the grave was born in Britain, one of the first generation of Londoners.

She was around 30 at the time of death so would have witnessed both the arrival of Rome and later Boudica's sack of the city.

no longer man nor woman…: Ovid, *Metamorphoses* 4.378-9.

BY BREAD AND SALT
Bloomberg WT 31 is a demand for money which contains the odd expression 'by bread and salt'. Roger Tomlin notes that it is probably an old-fashioned proverb, perhaps also used as an incantation against fever. It could also be a reference to a favour done for the recipient by the writer, 'the Roman equivalent of a free lunch'.

TO MOGONTIUS IN LONDON…
Bloomberg WT 6 contains the earliest written reference to London. Its addressee, Mogontius, has a Celtic personal name which, as Roger Tomlin notes, is also found scratched on a Roman clay dice from the Roman fort at Malton, North Yorkshire, in the territory of the Brigantes tribe (RIB. 2409.24).

The tablet's scribe appears to have had difficulty with London's (perhaps unfamiliar?) name, making its capital 'L' with two down strokes, as if written twice in correction. It is now on display at the London Mithraeum museum.

WILL
Bloomberg WT 48 appears to be the beginning of a legal Will. The Vangiones were a cohort raised from the German tribe of the same name.

THIEF
Bloomberg WT 59 could be a fragment of a legal document or even a curse. But, as Roger Tomlin suggests, it could also be seen as a tease between friends (or, as here, lovers). The tablet can be broadly dated between c.62–70 CE but pinned down in the poem to 69 CE, a disruptive year of civil war in which four emperors were appointed in rapid succession. In Britain, the governor Trebellius Maximus unceremoniously left the province after a legionary mutiny.

Myrmidons: Aeschylus's fifth century BCE tragic masterpiece which depicted the erotic love of the Greek heroes Achilles and Patroclus. The line quoted is based on fragment 135.

KEEPSAKE
(for Elena Theodorakopoulos)
A stylus, engraved on its four sides, discovered at Walbrook during the Bloomberg excavations. As Roger Tomlin notes, its message is along the lines of: 'I went to Rome and all I got you was this pen'.

THE HOUSE OPPOSITE
Bloomberg WT 14 contains only an address on the outer face of the tablet. It has been sent to Junius the Cooper, or barrel-maker, whose premises are identified by his neighbour Catullus, making the latter the earliest named householder in London. His name recalls the great Roman poet, Gaius Valerius Catullus, who was a contemporary of Julius Caesar and made rather derogatory mention of Britain in his verse, leading to the imagined connection with this later, British Catullus. The poem quotes a line from Catullus poem 11.

CATULLUS THE SLAVE
Bloomberg WT 70 documents a financial account made by a slave, Catullus, on behalf of his master, one Romanius Faustinus. Roger Tomlin notes there is no firm evidence this Catullus is the same person as that of WT 14 ('The House Opposite') but it seemed reasonable to venture an explanation. The poem quotes lines from Catullus poems 54 and 11.

ACCOUNT
Bloomberg WT 72 records the fragmentary accounts of a brewer or tavern owner (or both).

Agricola: Governor of Britain 77-85 CE, who mounted a campaign to subdue Caledonia or northern Scotland.

TOO FAR
(for Lesley Saunders)
Quote from Tacitus, *Agricola*, 29.
The historian Tacitus recounts how his father-in-law Agricola won a great victory at 'Mons Graupius', thought to be the Grampian mountains in the Scottish Highlands, although Tacitus was grieving for his son lost at the beginning of that summer's campaign. After the battle, the Romans withdrew and did not attempt a conquest of the Highlands again.

they create a wasteland...: Tacitus gives this line to the British leader Calgacus as he addresses his troops on the eve of the battle (*Agricola*, 30).

THE CAVALRY
Bloomberg WT 62, a loan note, is witnessed by three cavalrymen. The names of the debtor and the loan amount are lost.

THE CASE OF THE MISSING MULES
Bloomberg WT 29 contains part of a letter from a slave to their master recounting the complex tale of some baggage animals that had gone missing in their guardianship during transportation. Even the writer seems unsure of the exact details as they have written the name 'Taurus' over 'Taurinus' as a correction.

COINAGE
A writing tablet (RIB. 2443.7), excavated at Walbrook in 1927, appears to have been written by a businessman to his steward as he looks to cash in the value of a young female slave. The tablet gives no further details but here her home is imagined to be Nubia, an ancient kingdom of north Africa. The tablet is now in the British Museum.

II. THROUGH CLAY

AT THE TEMPLE OF ISIS
A clay inscribed flagon (RIB. 2503.127), excavated from Tooley Street, South London in 1912. Isis was an Egyptian mother goddess whose worship spread across the Graeco-Roman world, and was particularly popular with women. The graffito is the first evidence for the cult in Britain. The jug is now on display in the Museum of London.

Delos...Emporion: The Greek island of Delos was an early centre for the worship of Isis. Emporion (modern Empúries) on the Catalan coast of Spain was originally a Greek trading post. Fragments of pots with similar Isaic graffiti have also been found at both sites.

IN ATHENS
(for Paschalis Nikolaou)
RIB. 9 was found in Tower Hill in 1852. The Latin wording *na[tus] Atheni[s]* or 'Born in Athens' was added in much smaller lettering,

squashed between the final two lines, at the same time as the rest of the inscription. The stone is now in the British Museum.

CURE-ALL
RIB.2446.27, a set of four oculist's stamps, found in 1931 on Upper Thames Street is now on display in the Museum of London. Its stamps are written upside down on four sides so they could be impressed on ointment sticks. Although Tetricus the oculist has a Gallic name, the text contain Latinised Greek words, probably (faux) scientific terms.

CATULLUS'S BARREL
RIB.2442.21, a wooden barrel stave with a name stamp at right angles across its bung hole, was found in Bow Lane in 1960. It is now on display in the British Museum. See also 'The House Opposite' and 'Catullus the Slave'.

SEAFARER
RIB.3014, an inscribed slab found in Tabard Street, presents a fascinating mix of Roman and Celtic culture. It contains the first known use of the term 'Londoner' as a noun (Latin: *Londiniensium*). The rare Latin word *moritix* is apparently derived from a Celtic word for 'seafarer', and applied specifically to Gauls trading across the Channel between Britain and Europe. Tiberinius the seafarer's tribe, the Bellovaci, are from a Belgic area west of Reims, while Mars Camulus is a typical blending of a Roman god with a local Celtic deity. The slab is now on display in the Museum of London.

GOD HELP DEMETRIOS
A thin pewter strip, inscribed with a protective spell or 'phylactery', was found in 1989 at Vintry in the City of London on what would have been the Roman foreshore of the Thames. This strip would originally have been rolled up to be hung around the neck in an amulet case. Its text incorporates lines of Greek hexameter verse which were circulated across the Roman world by a sham Black Sea mystic, Alexander of Abonoteichos, as protection against the ravaging Antonine Plague of the late 160s CE (see Lucian, *Alexander*, 36). The amulet is now on display in the Museum of London.

THE MOST DEVOTED
RIB.10, a tombstone for a young boy made of imported stone, was found in Moorgate in 1911. His mother Eucarpia's name is added in smaller letters on the final line, as if the engraver had run out of space. It is now on display in the Museum of London.

BRICKING IT
RIB.2491.147, a red clay bonding tile, was inscribed with a graffito while the clay was still soft. The inscription forms a rhyming couplet in Latin which could have been based on a well-known quotation or possibly a popular song. It was found in Newgate Street, near the site of one of the Roman gates at the west of the city, and is now on display in the Museum of London.

CELSUS THE SPY
RIB.19, a large tomb, was found in Blackfriars in 1843. A *speculator* was a military policeman, or spy, probably attached to the governor's staff. Celsus's tomb is on display in the British Museum with a cast in the Museum of London.

our old legion… is split: In 196 CE the Augusta Second Legion supported the claim to the imperial throne of the then British governor, Clodius Albinus. This revolt was crushed by the legitimate emperor Septimius Severus.

THUMBS UP
Head quote from 'Death, women, and the afterlife: some thoughts on a burial in Southwark' by Nick Bateman in *Londinium and Beyond: Essays on Roman London and its hinterland for Harvey Sheldon* (London, 2008). Found in Great Dover Street, Southwark, the grave of a woman contains eight clay lamps, one of which shows a fallen gladiator. Three other lamps depict the Egyptian god Anubis, who accompanied souls to the Underworld, and was particularly associated with gladiators, leading to the suggestion that this might be the grave of a female gladiator (some archaeologists have argued for the slightly less sensational conclusion that she might simply have been a keen follower of the arena). The grave and its eight lamps are on display in the Museum of London.

missio: In Latin, this was literally a 'sending away' or a 'letting go' but for gladiators had the specific sense of a respite when defeated during combat – a thumbs-up.

HECTOR'S
RIB.2445.27, a child's leather sole, was found in a tributary of the Walbrook stream near the Bank of England in 1974. It is incised with the Greek capitals *EKTOPI* ('for Hector').

Ilium: The Roman city at Troy.

IN PIECES
Two large pieces of the altar tomb of Gaius Julius Alpinus Classicianus (RIB.12) were found in 1852 and 1935 respectively. Both had been moved from their original site and reused in Bastion 2 of the Roman town wall, north of Tower Hill. Classicianus was procurator of Britain after the Boudican revolt (61-65 CE), and credited with the rebuilding of the city after the disaster (see also 'Backfill') but apparently later forgotten. The blocks are now on display in a reconstruction of Classicianus's tomb in the British Museum.

AFTER THE FLOOD
Italic quotes throughout are from a series of six tracts and letters, collected in *The Works of Fastidius*, ed. R.S.T. Haslehurst (The Society of SS Peter and Paul Limited, 1927).
Followers of the British-born heretic Pelagius believed in the power of free will. Ancient sources record that the heresy was prevalent in late Roman Britain, and it has sometimes been argued that there might have been an attempt to set up a 'Pelagian state' in Britain following the end of imperial rule in 410–411 CE.

DARK EARTH
An archaeological horizon or layer of soil covering many sites of late Roman London. It is unclear whether its presence indicates abandonment or continuous occupation.

bears ran free: A fragment of a brown bear skeleton has been unearthed from the site of the London arena or amphitheatre at Guildhall, raising the suggestion that the rewilded arena might have been used for bear hunting.

FOR EVALUS, SON OF
(for Fiona Cox)
The huge stone in the porch of St Mary's Church, Spittal, Pembrokeshire, West Wales, is inscribed with the still-legible Latin inscription *Evali fili Dencu Cuniovende mater euis* or 'For Evalus, son of Dencuus, Cuniovende his mother [set this up]'. Cuniovende is a Brythonic Celtic name.

GHOST PASSAGE
(for Liam Guilar)
Based on Procopius, *On the Wars*, 8.20. 47–58.
Procopius recounts that he learnt this story from British travellers included in a Frankish embassy to the court of Justinian in Byzantium. It is possible that, hearing of an 'Isle of the Dead', Procopius might have confused the Greek for death (*thanatos*) with the Isle of Thanet which he might have seen on Roman maps.

A tiny carved cameo seal, dating from the third century CE and found on the Thames foreshore, depicts a ghostly Roman rowing boat with four sailors. It is now on display in the Museum of London.

III. ON STONE (OXNEY SONNETS)
(for Paul Dunn)

I. BULL
The altar, now housed in the church tower of St Mary the Virgin Church, Stone-in-Oxney, Kent, is carved with a bull and oxen. It was previously thought to be from a temple of Mithras but is now believed to depict the Egyptian bull god Apis, worshipped by soldiers across the Roman empire. It was excavated from the church nave in the early 18th century and probably came from the nearby Roman fort of Lympne. See also 'Block'.

II. WHITE
Head quote from Sir William Lombard, *A Perambulation of Kent* (1570).

milk moon: The full moon of May.
penitent: 'a spike or pinnacle of compact snow... left standing after differential melting of a snowfield' (*Landmarks,* Robert Macfarlane, Hamish Hamilton, 2015, p.89).

III. SHADOWTIME
In ecology, Shadowtime 'manifests as a feeling of living in two distinctly different temporal scales simultaneously, or acute consciousness of the possibility that the near future will be drastically different than the present' (The Bureau of Linguistic Reality: bureauoflinguisticalreality.com/).

The catastrophic winter storms of 1287 changed the coastline of Kent and East Sussex. The port of Old Romney was silted up and landlocked and the river Rother diverted through Rye. The town of Old Winchelsea was completely flooded and destroyed and is now thought to lie beneath Winchelsea beach.

IV. BLOCK
Reverend Culpepper Savage, thought to have removed the Roman altar from the church in horror at its paganism, was vicar of Stone-in-Oxney from 1716-1753. He had it placed outside the churchyard for use as a horse-mounting or, in Kentish dialect, 'jossing' block. His successor, Reverend William Gostling, restored the bull altar to the church.

VII. JAZZ
that spring night: On 15 May 1915, the first use of the term 'Jazz' may have come from Tom Brown's Band from Dixieland as they began performing in Chicago and started advertising themselves as a 'Jass Band'.

IX. IN INFANCY
Commission headstones: The Commonwealth War Graves Commission commemorates military service members fallen in both World Wars, either at their place of burial or as a memorial. Their distinctive standard gravestones can be found in many country churchyards.

X. VISITORS' BOOK
Seven 18th century oval text boards, with dire Biblical warnings, are displayed on the nave arches of St Dunstan Church, Snargate on Romney Marsh. It also has a fragmentary wall painting of a 'great ship' from c.1500 on the north wall.

www.ingramcontent.com/pod-product-compliance
Lightning Source LLC
Chambersburg PA
CBHW030048100426
42734CB00037B/583